How To Be A Wick In God's Candle

Learning to Pray for Others

Jim Rosemergy

For information, contact
Jim Rosemergy at jimrosemergy@gmail.com

ISBN: 978-1-365-60417-1

Other Books By Jim Rosemergy

The Watcher
The Gathering
The Third Coming
The Sacred Human
A Recent Revelation
The Transcendent Life
The Quest for Meaning
A Closer Walk With God
The Prayer That God Prays
Living the Mystical Life Today
Even Mystics Have Bills To Pay
A Daily Guide To Spiritual Living
Attaining the Unattainable, The Will of God
The Seeker, A Boy In Search of His Name

HOW TO BE A WICK IN GOD'S CANDLE
is dedicated to those who
seek to serve humanity through prayer.

Table of Contents

Preface

A candle is not a candle unless it has a wick. Even the smallest candle has the potential of providing hours of light and warmth. The only way to unlock the potential is to ignite the wick. The wick is not the wax; it is not the light or the warmth, but it is an integral part of the essence of a candle.

Imagine God's dilemma—an immense, immeasurable possibility of wisdom, healing and wholeness, peace, love, comfort and strength available to the people of the world—wisdom, healing and wholeness, peace, love, comfort and strength sorely needed. We cry out for God's help; we pray for others and ourselves. Some are delivered; others remain in despair. Grave problems continue for decades, millennia.

I wonder if a wick is needed.

This book is a call to humanity to become a wick in God's candle, to discover and put to the test a way of praying for one another that can transform us and the world.

This book is a call for us to embrace The Partner's Prayer prayed by our God.

> You cannot do it by yourself.
> I am not going to do it for you.
> Together, we can do all things.

Introduction

Beliefs evolve. In the mind of humanity and only in our minds, the world was flat; now it is round. The earth was the center of the universe, now it revolves around a yellow star that traverses a galactic center in a celestial neighborhood of 200 billion stars in a universe whose center is everywhere.

Once it was acceptable to own another person. Skin color determined whether a person was human or some form of animal. Due to the sin of Eve, men of Christian virtue believed women unable to serve the spiritual needs of sincere seekers of Truth. Some still do; others reject this belief.

How many different kinds of governance have human beings conceived in an attempt to bring order to tribes, cities, nations and the world? The truly wise create a governing document that can be amended by the evolving people it governs.

The cultures of the people of the world are filled with creation stories. The Bible reveals a Creator that brings the world and its creatures and plants into being through the Word. Another creation myth asks us to consider that the Creator dies and its body becomes the cosmos.

Beliefs evolve, and it is religion that resists the natural march of change with the greatest vengeance. Its battlements are dogma, and its highest walls are creeds. Tradition trumps common sense, and the wick in the candle remains unlit.

Section One

Preparing to Pray
Laying the Foundation

Chapter One
What If?

Beliefs about prayer evolve. They must. We don't know if the first prayers were cries for help or mumbled sounds directed to the spirit-world or thoughts that silently asked for what was wanted or needed, but a few things are evident. Prayer is viewed as something humans do in the hope of getting the attention of their God. Few of us wonder: Does God pray? What if we perpetually have the attention of our Creator? Would such a belief change the way we pray?

We believe prayers are words we utter, so prayer books are published, but some of us believe prayer is an experience of the presence of God and therefore cannot be captured in ink by the written word, whether it's on papyrus or paper or pixels on an e-reader. Prayer and ritual are often entwined, as the rising wisp of smoke created by incense is believed to carry prayers to a distant God. But what if prayer is not words? What if the words, whether spoken or thought actually prepare us for a prayerful experience?

Prayer has a direction, typically up; its focus is on a distant deity. We inform an omniscient, all-knowing Divine Mind of what It has missed. We strive to spur a reluctant, slothful God to action, to do what a good god would simply do; heal children, help the downtrodden, and stop the killing and genocide. Obviously, God is not doing what a good god should do; at least what we think should be done.

The result: people are angry with God, want nothing to do with the Creator or are convinced that God does not exist.

Perhaps it is time to change our ideas about prayer and the nature of God. What if our current beliefs about God and prayer/meditation are as outdated as the beliefs that the world was flat or that the earth was the center of the universe?

Prayers are usually about the world. We pray, God listens, and then God acts and fulfils our needs. This is our formula for a relationship between the Creator and the created. We need help with our needs. Healing is required. Money is crucial. A new job would help. A relationship needs healing. The other person needs to see it our way. Decisions are to be made. Peace of mind is needed.

But what if prayer is not about the world? What if it has a different purpose? What if there is no God listening to our pleas and prayers? What if God flatly refuses to do anything that God is not already doing and has been doing since the beginning. If there is a chance that this is true, it behooves us to discover what God is actually doing.

What if prayer is not about the human condition, as we have believed for eons? If there is even a slight chance that this is true, we might want to dissect our beliefs about prayer and the Divine in the hope that we can reassemble the pieces and build a new understanding of what prayer is and its purpose.

Chapter Two
Your Responsibility

It is natural to want to help another. We can provide physical help. We can mow a neighbor's lawn, bring soup when there is sickness, and shovel a driveway when it snows. We can be a listening ear or give gifts of money. We can hold a hand or place our arm on a shoulder. The ways we can help another are many, but there are times when we sense a transcendent power is needed. During these times, we turn to prayer.

Countless numbers of prayers are prayed each day. Names and needs are placed in prayer boxes and phone calls are made to powerful prayer ministries such as Silent Unity. Prayer rings are engaged in hope that the combined prayers of many support the needed healing or dawning of peace of mind.

Is praying for others a learned art? Are there principles to put to the test? Is there a science to praying for another human being? Are there laws and insights that are not consciously known that we are now prepared to see and practice for the common good? If there are such principles, how do we find them?

Jesus prayed effectively. Consider this episode in His life recorded in Mark 5:22-43. One day He was called to the aid of a sick child. As He walked to the child's home, a crowd pressed in upon him. In the crowd was a woman who had had a flow of blood for 12 years. She believed that if she could just touch the hem of Jesus' garment she would be healed. Undoubtedly, with great effort, she moved through the throng of people and touched His hulag, and her flow of blood ceased. Immediately, Jesus stopped and asked who touched Him. The disciples were puzzled because many people touched Jesus as He made His way to the side of the daughter of Jarius.

The disciples did not know that Jesus was not asking about physical touch, but who had touched His consciousness. In this instance, Jesus did not speak a prayer. He was simply moving through the crowd. This gives us a key to prayer and healing.

The little girl that Jesus was called to heal was dead when He arrived at her side. He found Himself not involved in a healing, but in raising a child from the dead. Imagine the consciousness Jesus was in as He travelled to the girl's side. He was not immersed in thoughts of death or there would have been no raising of the dead. I believe His attention was on life everlasting.

It was this consciousness that the woman touched, and in it there was no flow of blood. If we are to be helpful to people as we pray, this is the example we follow. We have a responsibility to give attention not to the person or their need, but to God and the truth of being. Remember, Jesus was unaware of the woman until she touched the hem of His garment, until she touched and was touched by the consciousness He was in at that moment.

There is another example of Jesus' consciousness at work. Read Matthew 8:5-13. A Roman soldier, a centurion, came to Jesus asking Him to heal his servant. Jesus indicated that He would go with the centurion to meet his servant. The soldier reminded Jesus that as a centurion, he was a man of authority and that when he commanded his soldiers to do something it was done. The centurion knew that Jesus needed only to command the healing, and it would be so.

This is an example of absent healing because Jesus did not touch the servant. The declaration of healing was given, and it was done. A consciousness of wholeness such as the one Jesus possessed knew no separation, no distance.

Are words necessary? There were instances in Jesus' healing ministry when He spoke and other instances when He did not. Sometimes He touched a person, but there were times when He did not.

It must be that words are not necessary and neither is touch; however, what is necessary? What purpose does touch serve? What purpose do words provide?

The best question to ask is what was present in each instance of healing? The answer is a consciousness of wholeness.

Let us return to the illustration of the candle. The most vital question is what is the avenue through which God's power is exercised? Remember the common ingredient in Jesus' healing ministry was not touch or words. The common ingredient present in each instance was His consciousness of His Father, His consciousness of Life and Wholeness.

This is our responsibility—to open ourselves to become conscious of the Presence. This awareness is the avenue through which healing and transformation take place; this consciousness is the wick of the candle. Our responsibility is to be open to this experience. The question is how can this grand responsibility be met?

Chapter Three
Foundation Principles

Our ability to make discoveries and evolve, not only physically but also mentally and spiritually, is a hallmark of humanity. Our understanding of the physical universe is evolving. We have discovered the link between space and time and now use a mysterious term— SpaceTime. Our understanding of God's name or nature has changed. Even school children note the difference between the wrathful, angry God of the Old Testament and Jesus' loving presence in the New Testament. A child remarked to his Sunday school teacher when the children began to study the Gospels, "God sure got better, didn't He?" Of course, God did not get better, but we are becoming more aware of the true nature of God.

Prayer is evolving and so is the way we pray to support and help others. In the past, we prayed to get God's attention and to call God to action. Answered prayer occurred because God acted. Other prayer practices emphasizing the power of the mind suggest to a person in need the answer to his challenge. Mental suggestion invites the person in need to change his consciousness and to see himself healed, prospered or illumined.

How To Become A Wick In God's Candle asks us to consider another approach to praying for others that is based on Jesus' healing ministry. The focus is not on the person or an attempt to get God to act. The transformation is initially not of the person in need, but of the person who prays. Certain foundation principles support this kind of faith-filled, effective prayer, so let us lay the foundation for the kind of prayer that calls us to become a wick in God's candle, so God's light can shine.

Each Person Is a Spiritual Being

We are spiritual beings living in a spiritual universe governed by spiritual laws, and we are having a human experience. However, nothing of the earth, nothing that has ever happened to us, nothing we have ever done has the power to change God's creation. We are as God created us—pure Spirit, pure Life, whole and complete. This is the truth of our being. So when we pray, we do so with the understanding that we are spiritual beings and that the people we pray with are likewise beings of Spirit.

Each Person Is One With God

We are as close to God as we will ever be, and the oneness is more profound than our words can declare. As the scripture reveals, God is closer than hands and feet and breathing. Jesus revolutionized spirituality when He affirmed, "I and the Father are one" (John 10:30). This statement caused those who believed in humanity's separation from God to take up stones to kill Him.

So when we pray, we do so with the understanding that we are one with God.

This realization asks us to awaken. Prayer is not about the world and our earthly ills; it is about awareness and a consciousness of the truths that are the foundation of creation and our lives.

We are to become aware of this oneness, and, quite frankly, it comes to us through grace and through waiting, as we shall see when we explore the prayer practice that helps us become wicks in God's candle.

The Kingdom of Heaven Is Within Each Person

Jesus revealed that the kingdom of heaven/kingdom of God is within us (Luke 17:21). The implications of this truth are immense. All we need is already present. It is once again a call to awaken, to be aware of that which is and therefore to live consciously.

There is a great potential within us. Of course, there is; we are made in God's image and likeness. Jesus proclaimed this potential when He said that we could do the things that He did (John 14:12). He also amazed us by commanding that we love one another AS He loved us. Once again, He demands, He commands, that we discover the divine potential that is within us, and that we express it. And it is best expressed when we serve others in prayer. Paul, likewise, discovered the divine potential within himself and affirmed, as did Jesus, that which is within us all. He wrote of a mystery hidden for ages and generations, Christ in you the hope of glory (Colossians 1:27). He wrote of his own experience, Christ lives in me (Galatians 2:20).

So when we pray, let us do so with this understanding: God has made a home in us; God lives in us and therefore nothing is missing, nothing is lacking. What is needed is present. What is needed is an avenue through which the divine potential can escape into our lives and the world.

Each Person Is Created To Be A Wick In God's Candle

All that is needed is present, the power to heal, ideas to prosper, strength to get up when we have fallen, wisdom to guide, etc. Our God is not to remain an imprisoned splendor as Robert Browning wrote in his poem, "Paracelsus." However, although we are created to be wicks in God's candle, a person in fear and who believes in separation is not yet eligible to be the wick.

In truth, the wick is not a person; the wick is a person who is awake and aware of the indwelling presence of God. This insight defines our work and shifts the focus of prayer. Rather than prayer that calls for God to act or for the person to accept a suggested truth or earthly condition, prayer's focus is to prepare us to be lifted through grace into an awareness of the Presence. The focus is not for God to act, but for us to be aware. Then God has a wick through which to shine, and the power that lies within is no longer imprisoned.

So when we pray let us do so with this understanding: We are willing to awaken and be aware of the presence of God that lives in us and that expresses as us. We are willing to be wicks in God's candle.

Be Still and Know That I Am God...

To be aware of God, we must be like God, and as Meister Eckhart said, "Nothing in all creation is so like God as stillness." Long ago, a Psalmist made the same discovery. "Be still and know that I am God" (Psalm 46:10). When we are still, we are candidates to awaken, to become aware and to live conscious lives. The prophet Elijah, fleeing from the vindictive queen Jezebel, found God not in the wind, or fire, or an earthquake, but in a still small voice (I Kings 19:12).

These recorded experiences guide us as we prepare to become wicks in God's candle. So when we pray, let us do so with this understanding: We become aware when we are still. We hear a still small voice declare, "I am God." We echo Jacob's discovery when He awoke from his dream of a ladder, "Surely God is in this place and I knew it not" (Genesis 28:16). And the place where we find God is within us.

These, dear friend, are our foundation principles. They are deeply spiritual. They are solid ground for the practical work of serving others through prayer.

Chapter Four
The Healer

In the smallest candle, there is the potential of hours of light and warmth. Likewise in each of us there is an immense potential of love, joy, peace, strength and wisdom, etc. yearning for expression. For both the candle and the indwelling Presence, a wick is needed. Although all of us are created to be wicks in God's candles, avenues of Divine expression, a person is not the wick. The wick is a person who is awake and aware of God's presence and power. Whenever this wick is present, the Presence has an avenue for expression.

This defines our work. We are to learn to be still and to listen to the still, small voice. As we wait, a dawning occurs, and an avenue is provided so the indwelling power can heal and help. Obviously, this requires personal transformation and spiritual awakening. We experience our true nature, and God has an avenue for expression. The divine potential is loose in the world.

This kind of prayer initially transforms us, not the other person. An avenue for God's expression comes into being, and the one we pray for is helped. Please note three things. First, we are not the healer; the "healer" is a consciousness of God. Second, what we call healing is actually wholeness appearing in the world. This "showing up" is natural. Three, God's way is always letting—"Let there be." Letting implies something is natural. We don't have to coax it into existence. Given the right conditions, it is made manifest.

Remember, and this is essential, God does not act through needs. If God did such a thing, as soon as a need arose, it would be met, but this is not God's work. The universe is created in a way that requires consciousness and awakening—ours. The divine impulse to express drives the universe; this is God's passion, but its instrument is consciousness, a consciousness of the One who lives in us.

Prayer workers are awake. God works through individuals who are willing to be awake, aware, conscious people. This is the divine partnership and co-creatorship that is portrayed in Genesis.

Typical prayer is an attempt to fix. The purpose of the prayer of the 21st century is not maintenance; it is to awaken and become conscious of the Divine and to realize who and what we are. In this way, God has a channel through which to do Its work. This is the heart of this new approach to praying for others.

In this consciousness of God, there is no fear, because there is no fear in God, only love. No disease, only life. No indecision, only wisdom. No lack, only prospering ideas and the courage to act upon them.

There is a wick, and God's light is shining.

Chapter Five
A Blueprint for All Prayer

Prayer is as old as the first human being with a problem he could not solve. In that moment, a prayer was born, and it, like a seed, has produced much fruit. The harvest from this ancient, prehistoric prayer, this first prayer, is profound for it has multiplied countless times. But if we are searching for a new approach to prayer, should we discard the harvest of long ago and strike off on a path where each step is mystery, or do we allow the grain from that first seed to grow again?

Let us plant the seed once more. Let our sickles harvest the grain again and when we look closely at the seed, perhaps we will find what we are looking for a blueprint for all prayer. Let us hold in our hands the ancient prayer that Jesus told us to pray, the one we call The Lord's Prayer.

Jesus the Christ etched in our minds a blueprint for all prayer. We call it The Lord's Prayer, but it is more than words to be spoken or sung. The blueprint is hiding in plain sight. It is our insistence that prayer is words that blinds us to the gift placed before us each day. With this blueprint, we can reassemble the prayer pieces and forge a new tool to help us build a life of prayer and eventually become wicks in God's candle.

Jesus was asked about prayer and He responded.

"Our Father…"

I think Jesus was saying, pray with the understanding that God is Father—that God is close at hand. Remember, the people of Jesus' day believed God lived in the Holy of Holies on Mt. Moriah in the Temple. The idea of God as Father was revolutionary. When we pray with the understanding of the closeness of God, prayers of separation fall away and prayers of oneness are born. Perhaps we join Jesus in His simple declaration, "I and the Father are one."

I think Jesus was saying, pray with the understanding that we are all children of the same God. When we pray this way, there are no prayers asking for victory in battle or for something at another person's expense. When we pray with the understanding, *Our Father*, we pray a prayer that could be prayed by any being in the cosmos.

Imagine how this understanding might help us pray for another. Perhaps we might hold in mind the following idea:

I am one with everyone and everything.

"Who is in heaven…"

I think Jesus was saying, Pray with the understanding that God is within you, for this is where Jesus said the kingdom of heaven or the kingdom of God resides. "…the kingdom of God is within you" (Luke 17:21). The source of this important insight lies in the structure of the Tabernacle, the forerunner of the temples of Solomon and Herod in Jerusalem.

When Moses led the Hebrews out of captivity in Egypt, their religion was born and began to develop. The people longed for a home, but it was important that their God have a home as well, so they were instructed to build the Tabernacle. In this Tent of Meeting, in the Holy of Holies, in the Ark of the Covenant, their Deliverer dwelled.

Each of the 12 tribes of Israel was assigned a place to camp—three tribes to the north, three tribes to the south and east and west. When a Hebrew awoke in the morning and faced inward, he saw evidence of the kingdom of heaven in the center of the encampment. Jesus, based on His experience, took this one step farther—the kingdom of heaven is likewise in the midst of each of us. We find it when we face inward.

When we pray with this understanding, we do not reach out to God, we look within.

Imagine how this understanding might help us pray for another. Perhaps we might hold in mind the following idea:

I look within and find the source of my being.

"Hallowed be Your name…"

I think Jesus was saying, pray with the understanding that God's nature, God's name, is holy, sacred, and good. Let us strike from our consciousness the thought that God is the author of war, famine, disease and suffering. God's nature is good.

When we pray, no matter the appearances, we remember God is good.

Imagine how this understanding might help us pray for another. Perhaps we might hold in mind the following idea:

God's goodness is the truth of my being.

"Your kingdom come
Your will be done
On earth as it is in heaven…"

I think Jesus was saying, pray with the understanding of how the universe works. God's kingdom first comes and God's will is first established within us, and then it is made manifest in our lives and on earth. As within, so without, on earth as it is in heaven.

When we pray, we give attention not to our goals and aspirations; we give attention to the Presence that lies within.

Imagine how this understanding might help us pray for another. Perhaps we might hold in mind the following idea:

*My awareness of the indwelling Christ is made manifest
in my life and in the world.*

(You) "Give us this day our daily bread…"

I think Jesus was saying, pray with the understanding that God provides us with what we need each day. This requires an attention to the present moment. We are not nourished by yesterday's truth or even the hope of tomorrow's harvest. Each day, each moment, is an avenue through which all that is needed is available. And please take note of the *understood* (You) at the beginning of this statement in the Lord's Prayer. I am uncomfortable giving commands to my God, but as we will soon see, an awareness of the (You) before several of these statements opens doors of more understanding.

When we pray, we do so with the understanding that the help is available now.

Imagine how this understanding might help us pray for another. Perhaps we might hold in mind the following idea:

All I need, I have. God is here.

(You) "Forgive us our debts
As we forgive our debtors…"

I think Jesus was saying, pray with the understanding that God does not withhold love from us. Instead, we experience love in proportion to the love we withhold or share with others. For instance, if we fail to forgive another, it is not that God refuses to forgive us. God is Love and where there is love, there is no need for forgiveness; however, when we withhold forgiveness or love, we shield ourselves from the love that is our very nature.

When we pray, let us do so with open hearts.

Imagine how this understanding might help us pray for another. Perhaps we might hold in mind the following idea:

My heart is open, and I withhold love from no one.

(You) "Lead us not into temptation
But (You) deliver us from evil…"

This is one of the most confusing statements in the Lord's Prayer, but when we consider an *understood* (You), there is clarity. I think Jesus was saying, pray with the understanding that God is not the problem; God is the answer. God does not put obstacles in our paths. God sends no temptation to us; instead an awareness, consciousness or experience of God delivers us from our challenges.

When we pray, let us do so with the understanding that God is not the problem; a consciousness of God is the answer.

Imagine how this understanding might help us pray for another. Perhaps we might hold in mind the following idea:

God is my constant help in every need.
A consciousness of God is the answer to every challenge.

"For Yours is the kingdom
And the power
And the glory forever. Amen."

This is more than a close or benediction. It is a statement of humility. Many consider this portion of the prayer an added benediction and therefore not a part of the original Lord's Prayer. This may be true, but if it was added, it expresses a humility from which we can all benefit.

And so no matter how we pray/meditate, let us do with the understanding that is at the heart of the Lord's Prayer. Let us not solely sing, chant or speak the words. As each word is etched in our memory, let us begin to see the blueprint for all prayer/meditation and the possibility of the life of prayer we can build.

Section Two

It's Time to Pray
The Wick Is Ablaze With God's Presence

Chapter Six

Let The Words I Speak Be Those of Your Own Heart

We tend to think of prayer as words. There are prayer books and written prayers in every language. There are ancient prayers that we memorize, but the work of prayer is silence. The good news is that words can support our journey into stillness and the presence of God.

We are discovering that prayer is actually an experience of the presence of God, but words can lift us up in consciousness and enable to us remain focused on the realm of Spirit instead of the world.

Words can reveal the state of our consciousness—our minds and hearts. We can initiate the words, or when we are still, words or thoughts can emerge that we have never thought or heard before. The infinite mind of God is pouring through us revealing the truth of being and the nature of creation.

When we pray for or with others, they expect to hear words, but the heart of prayer is waiting, trusting, stillness and silence. Words without stillness and silence are just words. Words with stillness and silence invite transformation, and the consciousness that unfolds can potentially become an avenue for God, a wick in God's candle.

The foundation principles we explored are solid rock upon which we stand. They are a wellspring from which we drink. They will give birth to our words and help us remember that unless we are spiritually awake, we are of little use. When there is no silence out of which words may come, the wax of the candle is present, the divine potential lives, but there is no wick and therefore no way for the divine possibilities to manifest themselves in the world.

We tend to think of dramatic miracles and speedy recoveries, but prayer usually transforms us gradually over the course of our lives. We pray without ceasing. We pray daily; we pray whether there appears to be a need for prayer or not. We pray because life is a consciousness of God and so is prayer. The wonder and joy is that each moment of reflection and inward turn helps create the wick that the candle needs. We are ready, and where we stand, when we speak, Spirit potentially can do its work and express Its perfection.

The person in need has a responsibility to ask, and to ask is to be open to the mystery of life. The person asks—the person in need is receptive—that is enough. His or her work is done, and our work begins.

Our responsibility as people who pray is to establish a way of life. The challenge before us is not the issue. The issue is whether our life is a life of prayer or not. Once we understand the need for the candle to have a wick, and that an awareness of God is the wick, our path is clear; we make ourselves available to Spirit. The consciousness to be transformed is not the one dealing with disease, fear or lack. It is our consciousness, the consciousness of the so-called healer. This is where God's work begins because without a wick the candle cannot radiate its light.

Our responsibility is to be awake—always—to speak the truth and to be still, so we can know God. To listen, so we can experience the Presence that is always with us and is the truth of our being. We listen for the words emanating from the burning bush, "I am that I am." Perhaps these words imply, I am all beingness, even the beingness of those labeled sick, poor or ignorant.

So if words are thought or spoken, they are always spoken in first person. Remember, the consciousness to be transformed is our own. We leave the other person be. He has asked. She is open and receptive; that is enough.

We do not consider their names, for their true name is I am. Remember our foundation principle. Each person is a spiritual being. We give no attention to their condition, for it does not declare the truth of their being. They are as God created them, and we want to be in a consciousness that knows this Truth, and what we must first know is who we are and why we were created—to be wicks in God's candle…just like everyone else.

It may seem that this approach to praying for others is egotistical. After all, the initial focus is self rather than the person or the need, but the truth remains: All that is needed is here, for God is here. There is power to prosper, to reveal wholeness, to illumine, to comfort, to strengthen, to prosper.

The wax of the candle, the potential of light and warmth is present, but there must be a wick. The wick is not a plea or a proposal presented to God. The wick is not a bargain. The wick is a person who is aware of the Creator; therefore the work is not to fix another, but to invite a consciousness of the One to dawn. Then the light and warmth of the divine potential begin to shine.

When we stand before a person in need of prayer, we listen as the individual explains briefly his or her challenge. As we listen, we determine the idea in the mind of God that is at the center of the person's deliverance from their pain, anxiety or problem. For instance, if the challenge is healing, the idea is life and wholeness. If a decision needs to be made, the answer will rise from the ideas of wisdom and light. Money challenges are met when we know the Source.

Plato wrote that ideas are the beginning of all things. Charles Fillmore, a co-founder of Unity, declared that ideas are pregnant with possibilities. Behind every challenge is an idea to be discovered. We give attention to the idea, and a consciousness begins to form out of which answers come.

When we are anxious, peace is what we want. "Just give me a moment of peace." As we center on peace, we might echo the words Jesus used to calm the stormy sea, "Peace, be still" (Mark 4:39). We let these words caress us and soothe our troubled mind.

So when a person stands before us and shares his/her challenge, we turn within to find the idea out of which the challenge will be met. Next, we say to our friend, *Let the words I speak be those of your own heart*. A series of affirmations and denials will flow from our prepared consciousness.

A few words about affirmations and denials. Generally, we assume that affirmations and denials are words. An affirmation like: *Peace be still my soul*. A denial like *Nothing disturbs the calm peace of my soul*. This affirmation and denial might be used together as we say to the person who stands before us, *Let the words I speak be those of your own heart.*

However, affirmations and denials are much more than words. They are two processes of life. Through our thoughts, words, and actions, we are always affirming and denying. Affirmation is the process of life through which we build up beliefs. Ideally, the beliefs are true, but this is not always the way it is. Often we affirm lies. We hold in mind thoughts that affirm we are undeserving or of little value. Obviously, as a prayer worker, we affirm what is true. This is where we turn to our foundation principles and the blueprint for all prayer we discovered in the Lord's Prayer. Our declaration might be as simple as *I and the Father are one*.

Denial is a process of life that has two applications. If affirmation says yes, denial says no. Ideally, we say no to error, but there are times when we reject what is true about us. The second application of denial is releasing, letting go or the cleansing of the mind and soul. Ideally, we let go of lies such as: Negative emotions rule my life. I will never amount to anything.

Nothing disturbs the calm peace of my soul is a denial because it says no to anything that disrupts our peace. *There is no lack in my life* is a denial. It says no to limited resources.

Affirmations and denials are often the tools of people who pray. We begin with an idea. We say no to lies, release error from our consciousness and say yes to life as we declare the truth. If a person has lost his job and fears tomorrow, we might give attention to the truth in the following way. Remember, it is our consciousness that first must be lifted up. *Let the words I speak be those of your own heart. There is no lack in God's universe. Through a grateful, giving heart, my mind and life overflow with the all providing abundance of God's infinite supply.*

What follows are examples of the uplifting words we might "pray" as a declaration of our willingness to become wicks in God's candle. These are affirmations and denials we might declare as we hold the hands of the one in need.

Please find a place for prayer and meditation and become still. Take a deep breath, a number of deep breaths, and then pause and observe your surroundings. Look at what is far and near. Look at the forms around you and the shadows they cast. What is moving? What is still? Do not label or judge or condemn what you see. Label not. Do not eat of the tree of the knowledge of good and evil. Call nothing good. Call nothing bad or evil. Just breathe and observe. Become the watcher.

And then listen for sounds far and near, those sounds that soothe and those that are loud or abusive. Each sound simply is…not judged, not labeled. It is…

After a time, let your senses begin to sleep and turn your attention inward. Continue to observe, to watch. Take note of thoughts and feelings. Do not judge them, label them or condemn them. No judgment, for each thought or feeling simply is. The result is a non-resistant state of mind, a meekness that opens you not only to your surroundings and thoughts and feelings, but, also, to the Presence. This non-judgmental time is for loving, loving yourself and all the thoughts, feelings, images and memories that emerge from within you. Do not cast them aside. Embrace them. Love them. Appearances may declare that these thoughts, feelings, images and memories do not want to be embraced and loved by you, but do not judge by appearances. All parts of you desire inclusion, acceptance and love.

If the prayer request is for healing, pray with the understanding. *I am a spiritual being. I am as God created me. Pure life. I am and remain under the care of the Great Physician. There is nothing to fear, for nothing of the world can touch me. I am pure Spirit, free, unbound. This I am and will always be because I am as God created me.*

And then rest in the silence and be still. Become the watcher. Observe the wondering mind. Some might say the mind is a wanderer, and therefore must be controlled. In the wick of the candle approach to prayer, the mind is allowed to run free. It is not judged. The mind is a wonderer. Let us discover what it is wondering about, and then after a time of observation gently bring it home again with a simple truth: *I am pure Life, untouched by the world.* And wait in the silence once more. Silence invites grace to take us deep into the kingdom of God. Our journey deeper is not because of our words or actions. Instead, something transcendent is our guide into the mystery of the presence of God.

Can you see the process? A wick is forming. There is the potential that Spirit will have an avenue through which to bring into manifestation Its creation, Its divine blueprint of perfection. The mind wonders, and we are the lovers we truly are, loving ourselves and all the parts of ourselves, because no one becomes a wick in the candle who shuns parts of himself or herself.

If the prayer request is for prosperity, we might pray in this way and with this understanding.

The manna is on the ground, the ground of my being. The 12 baskets of the feeding of the 5000 surround me. There is nothing to fear. There is no lack here. God is here, the Source of all. The Source is not coming to me. It is here. My heart and mind are opening, and the Source is pouring from within me. I do not want, for the Lord is my Shepherd and is my Source, and all is well.

And then stillness begins again. We honor the ancient call, "Be still and know that I am God." As the thoughts wonder, we wonder with them. We resist not. We accept the feelings that emerge. They are not good or bad. Emotions are not pushed aside; they are encouraged to rise up and be what they are. They have no power. God is the one Presence and one Power. Feelings are simply feelings.

After watching without condemnation and with love, we return to a simple truth and rest in the silence once more. Grace is coming. The mystery waits. The dawn of awareness of the One is near.

If the prayer request is because a person has an important decision to make, we might pray in this way and with this understanding.

I have the mind of the Christ. All wisdom resides in me. I am the light of the world, and the light of wisdom and knowing is shining. There is no indecision in me. There is no darkness or ignorance in me. I let the light shine. There is no decision to make; there is only a light to see. I am willing. I listen, I watch, I observe. I trust that not only is there wisdom to guide, but courage to act upon the guidance that comes. I let the light shine, and all is well.

Then rest in the silence. Watch the wondering mind. Sense the growing sensitivity of the soul. Return from time to time to a simple truth such as *I have the mind of the Christ* and rest in the silence once more. The wick is forming in the candle, and God has an avenue through which to shine. The spark will soon become a flame.

Healing is a great human need, but it is said that loneliness is an even greater challenge for humanity. We feel alone, abandoned and unloved. In subtle ways, a person's prayer request will often be for oneness and connection. If we sense that this is the heart of a person's prayer request, we might pray with this understanding.

I hear the ancient call, "Follow Me." I hear the whisper in my soul, "Lo, I am with you always." I am not alone. God is everywhere, equally present. Where I am, God must be. God is. I am awakening from my slumber to discover that I am a part of the cosmos, a part of everything—every tree, every bird, every mountain that rises from the sea, is a part of everyone, is a part of me. God is and I am. This is enough.

Rest once more patiently, humbly and watch the movement of thoughts and feelings. There is no condemnation, there is only love, so return to a simple truth and wait again. *God is and I am. This is enough.*

Remember that our focus is not upon the person, his or her name or the need. Our eyes are on the mount, upon God. This is not callous. We are united with all creation and everyone. However, we understand that there must be an avenue for God's power and that we were created (as is everyone) to be a wick in the candle. Our hearts are open to the one for whom we pray. Our hearts and minds are open to the presence of God.

Anxiety is another prevalent human challenge. Prayer requests may be for healing, but underlying the illness is often anxiety. When faced with this challenge, we give our attention to God and pray with this understanding.

Peace is my nature. Nothing disturbs the calm peace of my soul. Nothing of the world can change the truth of who I am. Peace be still my soul. Peace, perfect peace, is the truth of my being. In this peace, I rest and all is well.

Rest quietly and become sensitive to the interior world and the kingdom of heaven. If an uneasiness returns, turn to the truth. After a time of reflection and observation of the world outside and the inner kingdom, declare again: *Peace be still my soul. God is peace and peace is my essence. In this peace there is no fear...only peace, lovely peace.*

Relationship problems can plague us for years. Resentment, anger and hatred disrupt the calm peace of the soul. Hearts are closed and other relationships are impacted and influenced. Like dust on our shoes, we carry our issues from one relationship to another. We try to start over, but we are not new, so eventually patterns of the past resurrect themselves and unresolved anger and resentment intensify.

When faced with this prayer request, we give attention to God as love. *I am what I am. I am love's creation. I am made in the image and likeness of love. Love fills my whole being leaving no room for anger, resentment or hatred. My heart is open and I allow the love that I am to find its way into the world. I return to love and find I am one with all creation.*

I release resentment and guilt toward myself. The past is no more and love awaits me now. I accept this extended hand and silently rest in the quiet. I am more than healed; I am whole; I am love.

What if someone requests prayers for the selling of their house and the purchase of another house? What is the approach of someone who prays as a wick in God's candle? Perhaps the real issue isn't the house, but shelter and safety.

I let go. I am in the world, but not of it. I dwell in the shelter of the Most High. My home is God's presence and in this Presence, I am comforted and safe. There is no fear here; there is only God.

As is the case with every example of prayer, after the declaration of truth, there is rest and silence and openness to the presence of God, willingness for God's light to shine. The awareness of the Presence is the answer to the prayer and as we shall see, this consciousness does not remain in the abstract realm of the unseen. By divine decree, it is made manifest. (More on this in a later chapter.)

Prayer requests are nearly infinite, for we turn to God to help us with every human challenge. Let us look at one more example of the wick of the candle prayer process with a most challenging human condition—a runaway child.

When we pray, we do so with the understanding that the child is not alone, that the presence of God dwells within as a source of wisdom and strength. However, when we pray, we are consistent in giving attention not to the child, but to God. Remember, God is present, everywhere equally present, but the Divine still needs an avenue of expression. As people who pray, it is our responsibility to give attention to God.

I am not alone. I hear the quiet whisper, I am with you always. I am comforted as thoughts of separation and feelings of fear and worry fall away. What remains is what has always been, God, a God of pure love and peace. A God that is a part of everything and everyone. A Presence ever present, ever active. I am at peace, and divine order is established.

The examples above can be used in two ways. They can be a part of our personal prayer time dedicated to serving others. However, often we will be in the presence of the person in need. In those precious times, let us take hold of the hands of the person, and invite them into the prayer of the wick in God's candle. We gently say *Let the words I speak be those of your own heart.* We then close our eyes, take a deep breath and give attention to God and truth.

If we are a chaplain or member of a prayer ministry and know that we are the one "on duty" who will pray for others on a given day, our work begins at home before we leave for the place where we will be with those in need. There is much stillness and listening. The wick is forming, and it will be ablaze with God's light and love before we even leave our home.

In conclusion, in each example of prayer, God is the center, and an idea filled with possibilities expands our minds and calms our feeling nature. We speak or think the highest truth we know and then we wait. And, of course, the waiting is the challenge, and it is what we will explore in the next chapter.

Chapter Seven
The Challenge of Waiting

We are progressing and learning to pray in first person because if we are to be avenues for Spirit's work, we must come up higher. We take our attention off the problem and the person in need and give attention to God. We focus on the Truth, and then we wait. We wait for the awakening, an experience of the Presence out of which healing and various forms of manifestation come.

Our prayer practice is clear. We center on God, praying in first person and wait. When we walk the path of service, we quickly discover that waiting is the greatest challenge. The mind wanders, and we think we fail, but there is no failure; the mind is not wandering; it is wondering.

This realization is the beginning of learning to wait. Waiting requires love; demands love. Love, we discover, is the heart of prayer and meditation.

How we long for love—for someone to love us. Then we grow and long to love with an open heart, but it is hard to do because we cannot love another until we love ourselves. Remember Jesus' commandment? *Love your neighbor as you love yourself* (Mark 12:31). This is not a request. It is a statement of the way it is. We love others in direct proportion to how we love ourselves.

And so we try to love ourselves, and we "fail" until we learn to wait in prayer and meditation. When we are still, the mind wonders. Thoughts come and so do feelings. Images fill our consciousness, and distant memories are remembered. We think that thoughts, feelings, images and memories are intruders and try to cast them out. We resist them, judge them, condemn them, and we fail to love ourselves because the thoughts, feelings, images and memories are a part of us, ingredients of our humanity.

If we are to love ourselves, this is where we begin. If we are to love our neighbors, this is where we begin. This is where the loving begins, not in the world, but in the interior of the soul; and in some instances, in the darkest places in our souls.

The beginning of waiting is watching. Often we say, *I am a watcher. What I witness is a part of me*. Nothing is condemned. All is accepted. This is how loving begins—with acceptance. The first thing love does is accept what is.

Isn't this the way of friendship? Friends accept one another as they are. They don't demand change. They create an atmosphere that welcomes change.

Can we feel the gentleness of waiting and watching? Love doing its work, accepting what emerges in the soul. No labeling of thoughts, feelings, images or memories. Of each we declare *It is not good or bad. It simply is*. And then we declare the highest Truth we know and wait again. *God is, I am*. These six words are the beginning of loving ourselves. It is; God is; I am.

The qualities we admire most are not the qualities of our warriors, but of the mystics; the qualities that have mystified us for thousands of years: humility, patience, non-resistance, and persistence. These soul qualities begin to show themselves as we begin to love and accept ourselves and our innermost thoughts, feelings, images and memories.

Often we strive to express these qualities, but in most cases, we do not. The reason is that these qualities are developed in prayer and meditation as we love ourselves. They first live in us and then in the world.

Prayer is humbling. We try our best to focus on God, but our best is not good enough and never will be. Only when we adopt the stance *It is not I; I of myself can do nothing* do we learn the power of humility. Prayer/meditation is the best classroom.

We try to wait in prayer and meditation and "fail." Our minds return to the past and speculate or hope for the future, and the kiss of eternity—the moment—is unnoticed. We are impatient, but when we allow ourselves to be kissed by the moment, it is so full we find ourselves full of patience and enthralled with what is before us, with what is here and now.

Turning the other cheek and the non-resistance of such notables as Thoreau, Gandhi and Martin Luther King, Jr. are the great mystery of humanity. How can we not resist evil? Something must be done or so we think.

Where do we learn how to be non-resistant and uncover the courage to turn the other cheek? The answer—within us. Rather than resist thoughts, feelings, images and memories we consider irrelevant, negative, untrue or intrusive, we adopt the way of the mystic. When there is no resistance in us, our true selves emerge. We learn that the admonition, "resist not evil," must first happen in us. It is from this consciousness that we step into the world to do what is ours to do. This is not a world of two powers; it is a world where God is the only power. This is the world that Gandhi and Martin Luther King, Jr. discovered.

The Aramaic word for prayer means to set a trap. This implies that in prayer, we set a trap for God. Strange, isn't it, but I remember as a young boy how I set a trap to catch a bird. A box was propped up by a forked stick. A string was attached to the bottom of the stick, and I crouched 30 feet away—waiting and watching. This was most likely one of my first experiences of patience. I was persistent and focused and ready to pull the string and catch the bird. Are these qualities helpful in prayer and meditation? Are they some of the same qualities we just explored?

Here is the process again. We engage in our prayer practice of speaking or thinking in first person a declaration or an affirmation of Truth. We say yes to truth and no to lies and error. The prayer practice is filled with thanksgiving, for the consciousness of God is already established. The words or thoughts declare: *It is done. And so it is.*

For instance, if the need that turns us to God is healing, we might pray in this way: *I am pure life. There is no disease in me. I am completely filled with God. There is no room for anything but God. There is nothing aside from God. There is only God, and all is well.*

These words that become our thoughts are not focused on the problem or person. They are centered on God and declare the Truth that is eternal and always present.

We do our work. We prime the pump. Remember the pump in Grandma's back yard? There was always a bucket of water sitting next to the well. If there was a desire for the underground water to surface, the water from the bucket was poured down the well. The pump was primed.

Our affirmative prayer statements and denials are the water in the bucket. We prime the pump. We do our work, and then we wait as the inexhaustible flow of living water surfaces in our minds and hearts.

Here is the simple process. We become still following the guidance of the ancient Psalmist, "Be still and know that I am God." We affirm the highest Truth we know believing that it is already ours as Jesus declared when He said, "Therefore I tell you, whatever you ask in prayer, believe that you have received it, and it will be yours" (Mark 11:24). Next, we wait and watch and observe.

How long do we wait? If it is our personal prayer time, most of the time will consist of being still, silent, watching and waiting. If we are serving as chaplain and praying with individuals and there is a long line of people, the time of waiting will most likely be short, but nevertheless, there will be waiting.

As we wait, the mind may wonder. We watch and then re-center the mind with a statement like: *There is only God*, and then we reset the trap for God, and wait again. The mind wonders. We do not resist. We are patient, in the moment, and return once more to the Truth that is our center. *There is only God.* The pump is primed, and we wait once more. Perhaps we can hear the sound of the rising water.

This prayer practice is brimming with love, and we develop the soul qualities of the spiritual giants—acceptance, humility, patience, persistence and non-resistance. We learn to focus the mind and discover the subject of our wondering minds. We do not condemn the wondering. We accept the thoughts, feelings, images and memories that emerge, and eventually we find we feel much better about ourselves. We eventually love our humanity as well as our divinity. We no longer push aside the various expressions of our human selves. Guilt and regret diminish, and love pours from our souls.

Now we are ready for an experience of the Presence. A wick forms in us, and God's light shines. Those for whom we pray are served, and we declare, *Thank you, God; thank you, dear Friend.*

Chapter Eight
Letting Go of Outcome

Most prayer is about outcome. We pray because we want or need something to happen. In nearly every instance, the need or want is earthly: a healing, a job, rain, our house to sell or a house to buy, a decision, etc. This is understandable; life is challenging, but the greater challenge is to discover how life works, how the universe is designed, then outcome is assigned its proper place. Rather than being the center of our prayer, worldly outcome becomes an "added thing," a natural expression of a way of life rather than a plea or affirmation of what we think must be.

Jesus put forth the possibility that we can give attention to spiritual things (This will be defined shortly) and have our human needs and wants added to us. The idea was not original to Jesus. Other insightful people made the discovery. It is a revelation that is destined to dawn in each of us.

Jesus saw the answer to the challenge of life in Psalm 34:10. "Those who seek the Lord will lack no good thing." In Jesus' time people yearned for the coming of the kingdom of God or as it was sometimes called the Kingdom of Heaven. People struggling with life naturally thought that the coming kingdom was of the earth. There was a kingdom, so there would be an earthly king, a warrior and political leader. Jesus discovered and experienced a different kind of kingdom. He knew the kingdom was here; it was already present. This was His first declaration when He began His ministry, "The kingdom of heaven is at hand" (Matthew 4:17). He knew the key was awakening—to be aware or conscious of what is present within us—to have the eyes to see.

His call to us was and is: "Seek first the kingdom...and all these things (needs and wants) shall be added to you" (Matthew 6:33). This call shifts our purpose in prayer. It is not an earthly outcome; it is an awareness of the kingdom, the presence of God. How this consciousness manifests itself is none of our business. What will come into being in the world is added to us.

What a relief this is. Now we can declare, *Nothing needs to happen. Manifestation is none of my business*. We seek the kingdom, an awareness of God, and then take our eyes from our world and turn within where a greater sensitivity is required.

Let us see the process of how the universe works. Remember the Lord's Prayer revealed the answer. It is *on earth as it is in heaven*. As within, so without. As above, so below. All that comes into manifestation first resides in us as a state of consciousness. As we anticipate manifestation, we tend to look at the world, but this is not where a healing begins or the sale or purchase of a house. However, do not be discouraged.

As we wait and love all aspects of our being, the time will come when we enter the Kingdom of God. This happens not because of the way we pray or because we learn to wait. It happens not through our efforts, but through grace, the activity of God is our lives.

We enter the Silence. Our senses are asleep as well as our faculties of thought, feeling and imagination. We register no thoughts, feelings or images initially because God transcends thoughts, feelings and images. Remember, a thought is just as much a graven image as a statue of stone.

The Silence is without time; it usually lasts only a few moments, but this is enough to change our lives. We have touched the hem of the garment. We have experienced true Silence, a consciousness of the presence of God, and this consciousness like any other will manifest itself. Its greatest manifestation is our life, but rest assured that other things will be "added." However Spirit's first movement reflects the nature and character of God— intangible, unseen, invisible, and without form. We cannot see our God, but God is real and first touches us with thoughts, feelings, ideas and images. This is the Silence taking "shape" even though none of these four are tangible.

Each is without form. The nature of each is invisible. No one has ever seen a thought, feeling or idea. Even images are "seen" in an ethereal fashion. This is the way it must be because their origin is in God, in the formlessness of Spirit. Thoughts, feelings, ideas and images are likewise formless. They are intangible just like our Creator who gives birth to them, but the time is coming when the formless will assume its shape in our world. Imagine the idea of peace taking flight as a dove or a religion of oneness that calls itself Unity.

We engage in our prayer practice, we pray, and then we wait. Hopefully, there is Silence, but it does not matter. Our commitment is to be still and to seek the kingdom.

When our time of prayer/meditation is complete, we gratefully enter into our daily life once more, but our attention is directed inward as we first sense the movement of God in us. A consciousness is established that must take form in our world. (*On earth as it is in heaven*) We watch for it by being sensitive to thoughts, feelings, images and ideas. Then we look to the world and the realm of tangible events.

Usually the process of manifestation is like a pebble dropped in a pond. Ripples emanate from the center. In this analogy, the center is a consciousness of God, pure Silence. At first the "waves" are thoughts, feelings, ideas or images, but eventually they begin to take form. First, the "ripple" touches and heals the body. The innate wholeness is restored. It is revealed. The movement continues as we open our hearts, and relationships are harmonized. Next, job opportunities might be seen and steps taken to bring them into manifestation.

These are examples, but the possibilities are too numerous to recount. Remember, answered prayer is not of this world; it is a consciousness of God, and from this consciousness comes varied tangible manifestations, but not first. First, the invisible God moves in the invisible realms of our souls. Such is God's way...*on earth as it is in heaven, as within, so withou*t.

I love the story of the fiery furnace (Daniel 3:1-30). Three devout Jews were in captivity in Babylon. An egotistical king declared that when a musical tune was played the people must bow down to an immense statue of the king. The Jews who believed in one God refused to comply. They were brought before the king. He threatened them with death in a fiery furnace. In fact, he had the furnace stoked, so its fire was seven times more intense than it was before.

The three Jews, Shadrach, Meshach and Abednego, said to the king in Daniel 3: 16-18, "O Nebuchadnezzar, we have no need to answer you in this matter. If this is the case, our God whom we serve is able to deliver us from the burning fiery furnace, and He will deliver us from you hand, O king. But if not, let it be known to you, O king, that we do not serve your gods, nor will we worship the gold image which you have set up."

There is a message for us in this story. Shadrach, Meshach and Abednego released the need for a certain earthly outcome. For them it was important that they stand on their principles.

The good news was that the outcome favored them. They were put in the fire, but untouched by it. In fact, when they came out of the fire they did not even smell of smoke. Even the king had a spiritual experience, for he saw one like a son of God present in the flames.

This is what happens when we let go of outcome and stand on principle. We become aware of the kingdom or Presence that is always with us. The fourth one in the fire was the manifestation of their spiritual life, of their Silence. That Presence is made manifest in myriad ways. In the story of the three Jews, not only were they saved from the fire, but their faith deepened and they were given added responsibilities in Babylon.

Let us follow this example, and let go of outcome. Manifestation is none of our business. Who can predict how a consciousness of God will manifest itself? Let us experience the relief of knowing nothing needs to happen, for from this state of mind much will happen, but it will first happen in us. What is most important is that we remain true to who and what we are and to the principle that God is the only power in our lives.

Chapter Nine
Conclusion

Now is a time of choice. People have prayed for thousands of years with a specific outcome in mind. In most instances, the outcome was of the earth. For those following the prayer practice outlined in this book, there is likewise a specific outcome in mind, but it is not of the earth. Prayer is practiced, so the one who prays will become a wick in God's candle. The principle is that a wick must be present, so the Light can shine.

Remember the example of the candle. A candle may have the potential of hours of light and warmth, but the light does not shine unless there is a wick. When it comes to supporting others in their earthly and spiritual journeys, the wick is a person who is aware of the presence of God.

No one has the capacity to make this happen. We can only make ourselves available, but it is essential that this is our purpose in prayer and meditation. The changes that are made manifest in people's lives are as Jesus called them—added things. The wonder is that the wick, the person who becomes aware of the Presence, is blessed immensely. This is the added thing for the one who yearns to serve others in prayer and meditation.

So, dear friend, the choice is yours. Do you want to be a wick in God's candle? If yes, read on and let the next section of *How To Be A Wick In God's Candle* prepare you for the important work of service to humanity through service to God.

Section Three

Workbook
Questions, Exercises and Support

Chapter Ten
Wick of the Candle Workbook
Making the Ideas Come Alive

Your Day Has Come

Your day has come. This is the day you will serve others through prayer/meditation. People in need will come to you and ask you to pray with them. The day begins long before you take the hands of the people in need. You rise early and pray/meditate. You give attention to God. The following ideas are at the center of each time I am to be of service to others.

Here I am Lord. Use me. I of myself can do nothing. Through Christ I can do all things. I have the mind of the Christ; it is active in me now.

You arrive early at your place of service and the prayer practice continues. On this day, you do not interact with your friends. You are a friend to all, a silent wick in God's candle.

When a person requesting prayer approaches you, you hold out your hands and ask, "How can I help?" You listen intently, open to the idea that is at the center of the need.

If the need is healing, your focus becomes Life and Wholeness.

If a decision is before this child of God, you give attention to Light and Wisdom.

If there is chaos, you silently declare two words: Divine Order.

If there is anxiety…Peace.

If there is lack…Source and Daily Bread.

On and on the list goes with every human need being met by an idea in the mind of God. You are prepared. You are a wick in God's candle.

The time of prayer/meditation comes. You invite the person into the consciousness of prayer by saying, *Let the words I speak be those of your own heart.*

You take a deep breath, listen inwardly and declare what you hear. This is a key. You may speak the Truth, but it is God that speaks the Word. The Word is the Word of Genesis, the creative power God is. You declare what naturally flows into your mind.

NOTE: Many chaplains who pray for others are initially anxious and nervous. They fear that the words will not come. Everyone experiences this. The anxiety is a call for humility. There is fear and concern because we think we must do something. We have done much to prepare, but now is the time for trust and humility. It is not I... If a chaplain draws a blank (this does happen), he or she should return to *It is not I...* and wait. What is to be declared will be given. And remember, the words are not the prayer. Prayer is a consciousness of God. The words may reflect this consciousness, but the work is not ours to do; God's light is shining. We are simply the wick in God's candle.

The Truth is spoken and then you rest in stillness and silence, gently holding the hands of the person. If a thought comes to you, you might share it as part of God's gift to you both. Finally, you ask the person to take a deep breath and you say, *and so it is. Amen.* A hug can be given and the person leaves so another may come.

NOTE: After being of service to another, first time chaplains often experience a joy that they can hardly contain. This is normal.

Questions

1. Why do you want to be a wick in God's candle?

2. What is the Partner's Prayer?

3. What is it to touch the hem of Jesus' garment?

4. What is the responsibility of the person who prays?

5. Describe how the universe works in ten words or less.

6. What qualities are developed when we learn to wait?

7. How does Jesus' commandment "to love your neighbor as you love yourself" relate to your prayer practice?

8. Why are the following 6 words helpful when the mind wonders? It is; God is; I am.

9. Silence in prayer/meditation is not the absence of sound. What is it, and how long does it typically last?

10. Describe your prayer practice as you prepare to become a wick in God's candle. What do you do from the moment you wake up in the morning until you take hold of the hands of someone in need of prayer?

11. Why are humility and grace important ideas for the one who seeks to be a wick in God's candle?

True or False?

Indicate whether the following statements are true or false?

1.	Words without stillness and silence are just words.

2.	Answered prayer comes through our efforts.

3.	Prayer is a consciousness of the Presence.

4.	The heart of prayer is waiting.

5.	The heart of waiting is loving others.

6.	The heart of waiting is loving ourselves.

7.	Prayer establishes a way of life.

8.	Prayer is about the human condition.

9.	Prayer is words.

10.	There are no needs in God.

11.	The idea underlying healing is life.

12.	The idea underlying healing is wholeness.

13.	The idea underlying relationships is forgiveness.

14.   The idea underlying relationships is love.

15.   When experiencing lack, we give attention to God as Source.

16.   When experiencing grief, we give attention to Oneness.

17.   When experiencing lack, we give attention to money.

18.   When experiencing anxiety, we give attention to peace.

19.   When experiencing indecision, we give attention to the answer.

20.   "I have the mind of the Christ" is an idea to center upon when there is a decision to make.

21.   Manifestation is none of your business.

Multiple Choice

Indicate the answer that is most true.

1.   a. Beliefs evolve.
    b. Dogma evolves.
    c. Tradition trumps common sense.
    d. Prayer evolves.

2.   a. Prayer's direction is up.
    b. Prayer is words.
    c. Prayer is about the world.
    d. Beliefs about prayer evolve.

3.   a. A person is a wick in God's candle.
    b. A person who is awake is a wick in God's candle.
    c. Light is a wick in God's candle.
    d. God's candle does not need a wick.

Which of the following is not a foundation principle for praying for others?

4.   a. Each person is a spiritual being.
    b. Each person is one with God.
    c. The Lord's Prayer
    d. The kingdom of heaven is within each person.

What is false?

5.   a. God does not act through needs.
          b. Letting implies something is natural.
          c. Through prayer we fix problems.
          d. Prayer workers are called to be spiritually awake.

6.   a. In God, there is no fear.
          b. In God, there is no lack.
          c. In God, there is no disease.
          d. In God, there is ignorance.

What statement is true?

7.   a. Our daily bread provides for us forever.
          b. Daily bread is found on the ground.
          c. Daily bread is found in the moment.
          d. There is no daily bread today.

Complete the sentence, The Lord's Prayer is…

8.   a. A blueprint for all prayer.
          b. A prayer all Christians should memorize.
          c. Jesus' only prayer.
          d. Most powerful when it is sung.

What qualities are needed when we set a trap for God?

9.   a. Patience
       b. Acceptance
       c. Strength
       d. Humility
       e. All of the above

What is not a reason why we "fail" in prayer/meditation?

10.   a. Persistence
       b. Condemnation
       c. Impatience
       d. Resistance

When God first moves in your life as a result of grace and waiting, what can you expect to experience?

11.   a. Thoughts
       b. Feelings
       c. Ideas
       d. Images
       e. All of the above

What are the "added things?"

12.   a. Money
       b. Healing
       c. A relationship
       d. A job opportunity
       e. Ethan Allen bookcase
       f. All of the above

Exercises: Affirmations and Denials

1. Write an affirmation that supports a need for peace.

2. Write a denial that supports a need for peace.

3. Write three sentences that might be used to begin a time of prayer/meditation with a person in need.

4. What affirmations and denials would you speak while praying with a person for healing?

5. A person comes to you who has lost his job.
What idea is at the center of your prayer time with the person?
What affirmations and denials might you use in prayer with this person?

6. The person standing before you has lost her spouse. What prayer will you pray with her?

Answers

True or False?

1.   True

2.   False

3.   True

4.   True

5.   False

6.   True

7.   True

8.   False

9.   False

10.   True

11.   True

12.   True

13.   False

14.　　True

15.　　True

16.　　True

17.　　False

18.　　True

19.　　False

20.　　True

21.　　True

Multiple Choice

1. Beliefs evolve.

2. Beliefs about prayer evolve.

3. A person who is awake is a wick in God's candle.

4. The Lord's Prayer (It is a blueprint for all prayer, not a foundation principle.)

5. Through prayer we fix problems.

6. In God, there is ignorance.

7. Daily bread is found in the moment.

8. A blueprint for all prayer

9. All of the above

10. Persistence

11. All of the above

12. All of the above

About the Author

Reverend Rosemergy's journey in prayer and meditation began in 1974 when a classmate asked him to pray with her and sit in the silence each week before ministerial classes began. This prayerful beginning was in some mysterious way the seed for this book, HOW TO BE A WICK IN GOD'S CANDLE.

For over 40 years Rev. Jim has sought to support the spiritual awakening of the human family. He has served five churches and strived to help people as they experienced the challenges of daily life and walked side by side with seekers consciously desiring a closer walk with God. Through Sunday lessons, classes, special services, spiritual counseling and through his writings, he has encouraged people to discover and express their divine potential and to pray for others.

HOW TO BE A WICK IN GOD'S CANDLE is the culmination of his service and discovery of the foundation principles that enable any sincere seeker to become a wick in God's candle.